BETWEEN

Cruelty

AND Love

i

ZUBAIR KAREEM

BETWEEN

Cruelty

AND Love

ZUBAIR KAREEM

BETWEEN CRUELTY AND LOVE

Published by Pheasant Run
BCAL2013@yahoo.com

ISBN #978-0-9891073-0-3 Hard cover
ISBN #978-0-9891073-1-0 Soft cover
ISBN #978-0-9891073-2-7 E-book

Book design by Deborah Perdue,
Illumination Graphics

First Edition: April, 2013

Printed in the United States of America.

To my parents,

Who taught me by example.

CONTENTS

Introduction 1

Justice 13

Injustice 41

What is Ihsaan? 73

Injustice, Justice, and Ihsaan–

Putting It Together 87

Beyond Injustice and Ihsaan 103

Appendix 107

INTRODUCTION

*I*f given a choice, I doubt any able and sane person consciously and willingly ever accepts or agrees to an injustice inflicted upon him- or herself. We all may disregard a minor occurrence, especially if the price to obtain justice is high or if it is done by a friend or family member. This dislike or disapproval of injustice we have is not limited to that inflicted on ourselves alone; we usually have the same feeling if it is done to any other person, place, institution, or even idea we relate to or are associated with. It is also true that we like and prefer justice, especially when it is done to us or for us. We prefer the same for the people, places, institutions, or ideas related to or associated with us. These concepts are so universally basic and critical that every country and organized group of people has developed or adopted a set of rules and regulations to provide and maintain a system of justice. The system typically also provides some safeguards against mistakes and ways to settle any internal disputes. Even at a family or personal level, we tend to create and follow certain rules and understandings to avoid doing any injustice to each other.

This book is an endeavor to address these concepts: justice and injustice. It is a small and humble effort to help improve our understanding of these concepts, especially when they are applied to our daily lives. One might ask, "Do we really need to know any more than we already know about justice? Isn't it obvious?" or "Shouldn't we leave this subject to the legal profession to figure out?" I will try to convince you that it is very important for all of us to have a thorough understanding of the concept of justice. Not only should we have this understanding; we should also try to apply it to our day-to-day life and ponder it now and then. It is my hope that with this understanding, we might be led to an intellectual exercise that we otherwise might not have undertaken, and in doing so, we might rethink certain issues that otherwise have been difficult to work out. We might gain, in some situations, a better understanding or at least a different or a unique perspective even if we do not reach a solution satisfactory to our curiosity and mind.

One way to understand a concept like justice is to have a good understanding of what it is not. Therefore, insight into the concept of injustice is definitely part of the whole understanding of justice. Not only do I try to define and discuss the concepts of justice and injustice; I also explore some additional and closely related concepts—again, in somewhat simplified language and terms. I am neither a legal nor a religious professional or scholar, nor am I a preacher. From a religious perspective, I am a layperson. Since I was a child and for as long as I can remember, each weekly sermon I have attended has ended in the recitation of the same few sentences. These sentences encourage the listeners to be just and kind and not do any injustice. It is only recently though that I started contemplating the reasons and significance of these reminders. This was prompted by my experience in the local Sunday school. Not able to find enough qualified teachers for the school, the supervisor asked me to volunteer and teach a class. To my benefit, I agreed. The class usually included a group of mostly middle but some high-school-age children. After just a few sessions, I developed a renewed respect for teachers who regularly deal with this age group. I am not sure if I taught these children anything;

they and their parents might be the best judges of that. One thing is certain though, they really helped me to ponder and learn a lot. I could hardly thank them enough, even though I tried.

My concentration on the subject of justice is the direct result of a question that arose during a class and the discussion that came afterward. I cannot hide the fact that there probably was an element of longstanding interest and intrigue in my mind and thought processes for the subject. The questioning and discussion only rekindled it. What is justice, and how does it differ from injustice? How not-so-straightforward these concepts could be was an intellectual surprise.

The concepts of justice and injustice are definitely not new, especially in any legal discussion and terminology, and a number of books are available on the subject. What I couldn't find was a simple and straight-forward resource that I could use to understand, explain, and teach these concepts to children, young adults, or a person like me whose primary focus is neither preaching nor any practice of law or law enforcement. On one hand, I found that just emphasizing "being just" and repeating these words was not enough to have a full or what I would call a *useful* understanding, while, on the other hand, I also fathomed enough reasons for so much emphasis placed on this subject and its fundamental and universal nature.

It is important for me to state right here at the start of this discussion that besides describing justice and injustice in legal terms and concepts, I have tried to expand these ideas further to the concepts that might not seem related or relevant to what we generally consider law or law and order. Contemplating in this manner, molding this subject into a broadly applied concept, and expanding that concept outside the realms of a legal system, I found its larger applicability. In doing so, I was provided an opportunity to improve or sometimes reconsider our understanding of questions in many diverse areas—our personal lives, politics, many global issues, and even the "nature" all around us and beyond.

I take justice as a concept, an idea, or a notion, more than just an act, which might be the result of that notion. In this manner, it implies a particular arrangement of actions, ideas, or thoughts. In the larger scheme of things, it implies an analogous arrangement of material objects and even laws of nature.

Another important part of this thought process is that the concept of justice is considered to be not *unjust* on one hand but is also somewhat restricted by our intention to be *just* on the other. This particular understanding is an important requisite to understanding the scheme or model of the concept of justice and related subjects I propose in my later discussion.

Before I go into further detail, while we are talking about justice, we might ask ourselves a question: Could there be something, such as an action, concept, or ideology even better than justice? Something that we might say is better and beyond what we would call *just* in a particular situation, way of thinking, or action? I encourage the reader to think about this possibility while classifying an action, thought, or situation to be just or not. The answer to this question brings us to what seems like a novel concept. This concept and the word for it might be new for some readers. It is understood as *ihsaan*, which is native to the Arabic literature, pronounced like it is written, "ih-saan." It implies a level of action; an ideology, policy, or a situation that is better and beyond what we would call *justice*. I try to discuss this concept in detail in a later chapter.

I also try to answer the opposite question: could there be something worse than injustice? Logically speaking, there should be something, such as an action, concept, ideology, or a situation, that we might declare as worse than injustice. I labeled it *cruelty*. Here again, these words should not be taken merely for the actions they connote; they might also represent a certain way of thinking, ideology, and conception. Both *ihsaan* and *cruelty*, described in this manner, are discussed in detail in later chapters.

Now, if we look at the proposed scheme, we come up with the following figure. In this scheme, moving in a certain direction implies justice, while movement in the opposite direction implies injustice. The directions, left and right, taken in this diagram, are completely arbitrary and should not be compared with any political paradigm.

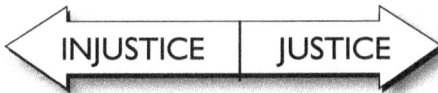

INJUSTICE | JUSTICE

Then I add two more concepts, ihsaan (to be elaborated upon later) and cruelty, to this scheme with ihsaan being better than justice and cruelty worse than injustice.

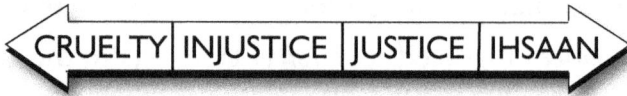

| CRUELTY | INJUSTICE | JUSTICE | IHSAAN |

Intuitively, one might argue that we should try to expand this diagram even further and come up with concepts on the left of cruelty and on the right of ihsaan as shown as empty boxes in the following figure.

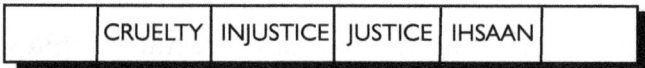

| | CRUELTY | INJUSTICE | JUSTICE | IHSAAN | |

I address this subject at the end of our present discussion and try to fill these two remaining boxes.

In the following chapters, I take each one of these concepts and discuss it in detail. I try to provide definitions of these concepts, if possible, or at least come up with a few examples where these concepts could be applied, the way I understand them, and so comprehended.

JUSTICE...

*L*et us try to understand the concept of *justice*. Within the life forms we are aware of, and at least the way we generally understand it, justice seems like an exclusively human concept. It might have been inherent to us or might have originated at a certain level of our familial or tribal organization when the need for such a concept was envisioned. Practical and social benefits achieved with its practice probably became the driving force behind its widespread appeal and application. However, difficulties remain with its universal application and even its definition.

It might be easier to understand the concept of justice if we envision it in legal terms. This way, we might say that justice is what is "fair," provided we are able to define what "fair" is in a particular situation. If somebody steals my car, he has not only to return the car but also pay a fine or go to jail. Somehow, we have determined that returning the car alone is not *just* enough. The added requirement of a fine or incarceration is considered fair in a situation like this. But what if the person who stole my car was in a precarious situation? What if he was going to lose his life or could miss an opportunity to accomplish a task with a larger purpose beneficial to the society as a whole and had no other choice but to take over or steal my car? In that situation, returning the car alone might seem "fair" and a fine and incarceration might seem "unfair."

"Fair" to some might mean "equal value," but the concept of value might be different for different people and in different situations or locations. The value of one hundred dollars for somebody who makes thousands in a month is different than it is for another working at a minimum wage. Let's say they both are guilty of a minor crime requiring a fine of one hundred dollars. While the fine is of equal value, it does seem a little unfair to one of them.

The equal value principle is also not applicable in all situations. Let's take the example of one person killing another person. Taking the life of a person convicted of murder is an age-old human tradition. Applying it universally though, without any context, is deemed to be unfair or unjust. In some situations, depending upon the nature of the crime, the intent, and the means involved, the death penalty seems to be appropriate. We might be justified to grant the death penalty to a man who follows a jogger to her home, makes a forcible entry, rapes her, and kills her. We might not consider that for a woman who loses control of her car and hits and kills an old man walking on the street. The decision, in this case, is based upon the intention and motives of the person involved, not merely on his or her action.

In the context of schooling, the children of a privileged race or social group of any society would likely insist on equal value being given to a standardized test score for a prestigious college admission, while the disadvantaged or discriminated-against group, especially if there is a marked difference in schooling resources and facilities, might consider it unfair. If a factory is being considered to be built on a riverbank with some potential of environmental harm, especially to the river water, opinions can differ between people living up- or downstream. It might not be fair to give equal weight or value to the opinion of people living upstream even if they out-number the other group. However, some people might declare this way of thinking unfair. Defining the concept of fairness can be a difficult task; it potentially can be easily con-strued in a number of ways because of political or selfish interests.

Another way to look at the concept of "fair" might be to expect people to do what you or I would do if we were put in that situation, but this approach could make things complicated because of our personal biases. If somebody hit our car while coming out of a driveway, we would expect that person to contact us and settle. Is that because we would do the same if we were in that situation? Maybe, but we might not; in fact, many of us don't do that at all.

Another way to understand justice is to understand what a "good" action or ideology is. But the concept of "good," for a particular situation, might require a discussion. A bottle of milk is good for a baby, but breast milk might be better. A serving of milk, bottle or the breast, is good for the same hungry baby but might not be good if given every hour. A serving of honey might be good for you, but the same serving at each meal might not be, especially if you are diabetic or obese. Financial help from the state could be good for me if it is temporary, for a short while, until I find a different means of employment or a new job, but not if I make it a livelihood. The Taser use could be a good option for police to control an attacking person but not if used to control a protest. Building a strong military to protect the country is good, but using the same force to control or colonize others is not—and even worse when it starts controlling its own people. Something that is seemingly or apparently good, without a pertinent control, could easily and very well lead to an unjust outcome.

Let's look at yet another way of defining justice; justice is the "right" thing to do in a particular situation. But just like "fair," "right" is also not easily definable. Our government, directly or indirectly, gives billions of dollars of tax subsidies to oil companies, which have been raking in many more billions in profit. For some, it is the right thing to do to ensure cheap fuel and further local innovation, exploration, and employment in this field. For others, it is absolutely wrong and is the cause of a number of problems we and the world are facing. For a long time, we have been giving subsidies to farmers—the right thing to do, according to many of us, to ensure a certain level of farm production, a need and basic necessity. But, for many, there is enough evidence to doubt this assertion. In recent times, the producers of ethanol from corn and the corn growers are the beneficiaries of the government subsidy. This subsidy provides us with an excess crop of corn, which is used to manufacture ethanol that is added to the fuel we put in our cars. This fuel, unlike gasoline, is biodegradable and, according to some estimates, produces less of the greenhouse gases. Also, it does somewhat lower our reliance on foreign oil. The subsidy to corn growers seems a right thing to do, except that many disagree and provide counter-arguments. On one hand, this policy has raised the price of corn, which has affected the price of tortillas, a staple for many less privileged, and a variety of other food items we all need on a daily basis. On the other, with a swath of land and machinery available to our farmers, an excess of corn by-products in the world market can practically threaten the sustenance of many small farmers all over the globe. Even the environmental benefits of this policy, if we take the whole farming process with its present and future cost to the land and environment into consideration, are somewhat debatable.

Defining what is fair or right might not be that easy and is subject to the biases created by our own interests and ideologies. To avoid such biases, to a certain extent, we try to devise a system of rules and regulations. But the conception, development, and modification of the system of rules and regulations itself is subject to maneuvering, for one reason or another, by the people in charge to an extent that it may easily lead to covert or overt injustice.

Finally, we need to discuss the issue of the intention of an act or ideology. We cannot ignore the intention of an ideology or action before reaching any verdict about its justness, but we also cannot make our decision solely based upon the intention either. First of all, a person's, group's, or government's real intention can sometimes be quite difficult to fathom. Even if the intention is clearly stated or known, misrepresented, misplaced, or wrong intentions can definitely lead to widespread or gross injustice. In fact, even with all the good intentions, some policies and ideas could end up causing more injustice and harm than benefit to the cause of justice.

It is not uncommon for governments, including our own, when dealing with a restive law-and-order situation, to promulgate and pass some kind of security legislation, which on face value seems harmless and protective of our lives and livelihood. The intention of the people involved in such legislation may or may not be clearly stated or understood but usually remains mostly unchallenged. The ruling class or the government, representing the majority or the minority of the society, depending upon the type of government involved, in the name of justice, with their "good" intention to provide security could end up causing gross acts of injustice.

Some argue that one really has to be somehow completely unbiased and unattached to a situation to find a fair or just solution for a problem or a dispute. All possible or relevant sides of an argument have to be weighed at an equal level before making a decision. Though the concept is logically attractive, in reality, it is difficult if not impossible.

In legal proceedings, juries and judges are expected to be completely unbiased while giving their opinion. Enough effort is usually made to make that possible. But does it really happen? Is it really possible for a human being to be completely unbiased about a situation? You might say, it depends; one could be unbiased if the decision he or she is going to make would not affect him or her in any foreseeable manner. Let's say we are asked to make a decision about a dispute between two parties in a distant society. For the purpose of discussion, let's believe that we do not have any direct or indirect interest in the outcome of the dispute. It seems that we could very well be unbiased in such a situation. But the mere fact that we are not part of the society with which we are concerned and about which we are asked to give an opinion might create a significant bias.

We tend to make decisions based upon our own way of thinking, values, experiences, and rules. In a pure legal sense, even for issues as universal as, let's say, human rights, we, in the eyes of each other, could very well be biased.

Bias can originate from multiple sources and can take many forms. Three types of bias are worth mentioning here: The first type might be called a personality bias. It is because of the peculiar nature or characteristic of the person(s) involved. For an example of this type of bias, let us look at a typical architectural design competition for a building. The jury might review the initial proposals without knowing the identity of the designers, as much as possible, to do justice to all designers. This continues up to a certain level when a few designs might be selected from the group. The next step of the competition when the designers might be asked to explain their designs carries the risk of subject bias. One architect might not be as skilled in presentation as the other one, even if his design is better. A well-established and respected architect might get a more favorable response than an amateur one. Similarly, it might be difficult to challenge the opinion of a senior professional, even if it is wrong. These examples might suggest an inappropriate favor to the person involved in this situation; in many other situations, it could be a hindrance. A person from a different society or culture, a different financial or social class, or who does not look like us or does not speak our language could be at risk of this type of bias.

The second kind of bias comes from the nature of the subject or the issue under consideration. In a recently held referendum in Oklahoma, 70 percent of voters approved a measure that barred local courts from considering a foreign religious law in deliberation. Now, there is a strict, well-defined, and established clause in our constitution that precludes our government or courts from favoring one religion over another or any religion for that matter. The drafters of this measure were trying to bar Islamic law specifically. The nature of this particular issue, for a number of reasons beyond the scope of this discussion, biased the majority's view, and the measure was overwhelmingly passed.

The third type of bias is procedural bias, which originates from the procedure employed to resolve an issue. A good example of this, in legal proceedings, could be the establishment of military courts, which are usually set up during wartime, avoiding the standard civilian court system. No amount of explanation or justification can hide the fact that, in any country, including our own, these courts are not the same as the civilian courts, the ones we refer to if we are looking for justice, and thus carry an inherent bias.

The concept of procedural bias, in a different way, is also well known in scientific research. Scientists know that even a minor change in the scientific methodology or environment can sometimes significantly skew an experiment's results. Even if done precisely in an identical manner, the results might not be exactly the same. There could be variables the experimenter is not aware of or not able to control at the time of the experiment. As long as the results fulfill a reasonably expected level of correctness, we accept them. Removing all bias and doing complete justice to the experiment, which might mean not favoring any one position or the other, or to achieve an absolute level of accuracy, in this context, is seldom possible. How much room we have to waver without being inaccurate or unjust depends upon the nature of the experiment or the subject matter. While a meteorological scientist might be doing justice to his job if the methodology he uses to come up with the weather prediction is correct nine times out of ten, a pathologist analyzing a tissue specimen to determine if the patient has any cancer or not has to be much more accurate to earn that distinction.

To come up with a just conclusion of an argument or an issue, we have to remove or minimize all of these three or any other types of biases. In reality, this goal is hard to achieve, if not unattainable. The level of justice achieved is inversely proportional to the amount of bias in decision making one is dealing with.

The relationship between justice and the organization and order of things is also interesting to look at. Actions and ideologies that follow rules of justice lead to more or long-term order and organization in a system. On the other hand, unjust actions or ideas culminate in disorder and disorganization. This does not mean that there might not be a well-organized system to cause or inflict injustice or the injustice never leads to any order. What I am saying is that this so-called order, a product of injustice, in a larger scheme of things, leads to a greater level of disorder and chaos. A dictatorial system of government, especially with a strong military imperium usually becomes a well-organized and orderly system. In almost all cases, at least in the longer run, however, it leads to a greater level of injustice, disorder, and chaos. In the last century of our existence, we have had numerous such examples in almost every continent we study.

Representative and democratic types of government can also be equally short-sighted and indulge in activities and legislation that seem to give a false impression of an order or organization but in the longer run, similar to the dictatorial system, could be thoroughly unjust and a source of suffering, mayhem, and turmoil. Declared or perceived states of war typically create such circumstances. Other reasons include social, cultural, and religious differences within the groups of the same country or society. It is also true that in a well-established democratic system of government, for its own population, these practices might not surface until a perceived social crisis or a war. In less well-developed systems, there could be a number of other excuses.

Instead of figuring out what is "fair," "of equal value," or "the right thing to do" in a particular situation, we may judge our actions or ideologies as they relate to an already decided upon set of rules. For example, for a murder, one could be given a life or long-term imprisonment or a death sentence. For a legislator—and for that matter, maybe for most of us—justice, in the case of a murder, might mean or require reaching one of these two goals. For a legislator in Texas, in such a case, justice requires imposing a death sentence on the murderer; while in Massachusetts, it might mean life imprisonment. In either case, they are reaching this conclusion based upon a previously made decision or a rule. For them and each body of citizenship of these states, the position taken by the other might be perceived as either unjust or not just enough.

While making a decision about any significant matter, a number of factors affect the way we come up with the final opinion or a judgment. It is fair to say that the ability to think critically varies tremendously among us. Many of us see things in the light of our life's experiences. Some of us follow a religious or a so-called "ethical" code or way of thinking;

others have a personal or political paradigm or a "guru" or mentor, and yet some others favor a particular subject or an issue through which everything else is measured, the so-called "litmus test."

The issues we deal with could also be quite complex, both ethically and scientifically. In the following paragraphs, I provide a few examples of some difficult issues and concepts of our times and try to suggest a course that seems just to me.

If you take a human egg and a sperm and let them join, in the fallopian or test tube, and provide them with a favorable environment, chances are the resulting cell, the human embryo, will start replicating. This would start a process that could ultimately lead to the development of a human being. If the concept of life is the ability to grow and the capacity to perform certain chemical reactions that may lead to propagation and reproduction, the embryo has a life. At what stage could this life be called a human though?

Some say that life starts at conception; for them, a human embryo is a human being. Others believe that human life really starts much later, maybe when a live human being is born. The debate about this issue is usually not scientific but could be equally difficult if it was. The controversy and considerations are really religious and/or ethical.

Are the wildflower seeds I am keeping in my garage, waiting for the spring thaw, living beings? In them, the plant's sperm and eggs have already joined. Scientifically speaking, they are not unlike human embryos stored in a freezer. They could also start growing and propagating if I put them in my yard at a proper time. The difference really is ethical: plant versus human being.

It is not uncommon for a woman to have a miscarriage when, for a number of reasons, an embryo or a fetus is naturally aborted. In most cases, in a purely religious or ethical context, we don't regard it the way we do the death of a living human being.

In human development, ethically and sci-entifically speaking, especially in terms of present-day biotechnology, we may figure out a stage at which a fertilized human egg has a definite chance of becoming a human being, a point of no return. We could try to be, based upon our present understanding of human physiology, as precise as possible. I say that, in nature, that stage is reached once an embryo is implanted in its proper place, the uterus of a human being. Without this step, it may survive and even divide but may not be able to grow into a living human being. After implan-tation, all ethical considerations may apply. Before that, it could have a different desig-nation, an entity with multiple potentials, depending upon the environment it is provided. Justice in this case could be to sensibly legislate the policies and practices dealing with this entity and its uses.

Let's continue this discussion further and discuss a different matter. Is abortion a just act? It might be, if performed to save a mother's life. It might also be just in some other situations, such as when we have the proper knowledge of a serious malformation or an ailment affecting the fetus. In the case of a rape, it is not an easy matter to settle. Agreeing with the victim's wishes in this case would be more just than not. Abortion, as a routine procedure, is injustice, and in some cases, it is even worse. Some argue against abortion in any circumstances, based upon their "pro-life" philosophy, stating that it takes a human life, a life that never really came into a conscious being. But the same people may not disagree with taking a lot of other human lives, which undoubtedly came into being, for one reason or another. As we allow taking a human life for our desire and justification to be just for the life that is ours or that already exists, we are unjust putting absolute restrictions on abortion.

Can a war ever be just? Like an abortion, it might be. A just war is for a cause, a just cause, not to annihilate the enemy. A war of occupation or of an undeclared covert cause is a very unjust war. Every war has a terrible human and material price; it is high if it is lost, but exponential if it was unjust.

A just war is conducted in a just manner. In spite of our presumptuous intellectual development and the lessons we learned during the twentieth century, present-day warfare continues to incorporate flagrant violations of basic human values, indiscriminate killings, and systematic torture or punishment of innocent men, women, and children. Justice remains the first casualty of any war. Armies of men and women, instead of their community leaders, continue to dictate the course of any conflict. People continue to forget that wars are seldom won by generals; they only win battles. Unless we address, investigate, and mitigate the injustices of our own policies, decisions, and forces in action, no war will ever lead to an enduring and meaningful peace.

What about freedom? Is freedom a right or a privilege? It seems a right if one lives in New Hampshire but a privilege for a Palestinian. What makes a society free is not its wealth, its size or numbers, or even its military prowess; freedom comes only with justice. Our leaders tell us that they intend to bring freedom to distant nations. Without halting the unjust means of their own operations, it remains only a slogan.

Smoking has long been known to cause health problems, including the possibility of lung cancer and death. In an interdependent society where the health cost is borne by the society in general, it is perfectly valid to suggest that smoking cigarettes by an individual is as unjust to the society as its sale to the general public. We have laws somewhat restricting cigarette sales and an elaborate taxation structure to cover the cost of associated health care. But then, what about alcohol? It also causes devastating health problems and disabilities. In Massachusetts, the tax on a pack of cigarettes is many times higher than the tax on a six-pack of beer. Are we doing justice only targeting cigarette companies?

The purpose of this discussion is not to give an impression that justice is impossible to achieve but rather to emphasize the fact that at times it is difficult to define with precision. Impreciseness is an important aspect of the definition of justice and justice itself. Ideally, it does not define where the line for "black" or "white" or "right" or "wrong" should be; it only tries to delineate the extent of each. Its scope is not precisely demarcated. Sometimes, it is narrow and fast like a river rushing through constricted valleys and rugged canyons, and at other times, it expands like a large, leveled watercourse. For social justice to take place, one could be deprived of his resources or rewarded, punished or pardoned, imprisoned or set free, or even killed or saved.

Justice is not a clear-cut line between two different opinions or ideologies. It is rather a sometimes difficult to define but definitely flexible phenomenon. It is a spectrum of actions and ideologies instead of a single spot.

INJUSTICE...

*I*njustice is also easier to understand if taken purely as a legal concept, but taken that way, I believe, its philosophical scope seems restricted or not readily comprehensible. To have a better understanding, especially of its larger application, we need to expand it to the concepts typically outside the practice of law. In this manner, it helps us to dwell on certain subjects from a somewhat different angle and might provide us with an opportunity to find a clarification or reach a solution, if there is any, to our satisfaction.

In simple, abstract terms, injustice is what beauty tries to overcome.

It is interesting to analyze what exactly the meaning of somebody or something being beautiful is. It is true that we might have our own individual perception of beauty, but there is enough overlap. There are certain things or places that are beautiful to most, if not all, of us. It is quite possible that things or entities that are beautiful, especially over a longer period of time, to our eyes share some common elements. The opposite is also true. A poorly designed building, structurally or aesthetically, is injustice by a professional. Dilapidated houses and deteriorated streets, either in the slums of our own cities or any other city in the world, are as unjust to their surroundings as the suffering of their residents.

Injustice is an act, policy, or ideology that, if it occurs or is implemented, leads to an undeserved physical or emotional harm and discrimination or annexation of due rights. It leads to a situation with harmful consequences to the subject, which could be a person, any other living being, or even a nonliving object or an idea.

The most widespread form of injustice probably is hiding the truth and/or lying. Its effect is never really positive and cannot be balanced by any number of subsequent attempts at its justification. Lying to obtain a personal benefit or a favor is injustice; hiding the truth that could prevent somebody from physical, emotional, or fiscal harm is cruelty. Can a lie ever not be wrong or a truth not be right? Ideally, never!

An unjust action or a practice leads to an ugly, impractical, or harmful outcome. Unjust ideologies and philosophies produce inappropriate or unnecessary suffering and systemic disorder and chaos. Some common causes of injustice are ineptness, insecurity, selfishness, exploitation, and greed for power and resources. The purpose—and thus the effects—

of an unjust action or ideology is distortion of facts and truth, benefit without justification, disturbance of rhythms and beauty, and deprivation of due rights. Its scope and intensity could vary depending upon the level or the direction it takes or its conceptual distance from justice, as delineated in this diagram:

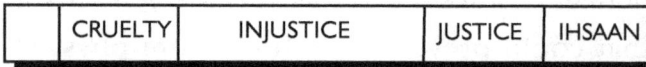

	CRUELTY	INJUSTICE	JUSTICE	IHSAAN

If a school's policy is to enroll students based purely on a test score, irrespective of their race or gender, and it denies admission to a student with a higher test score and enrolls somebody for an alternate reason, the school's action could be deemed unjust. Similarly, in a system like this, if a whole group of students are systematically deprived of an appropriate educational environment and level of instruction, compared to the folks just across the zip code, the whole admission process might have the same flaw.

Some might say that this kind of reasoning in itself is unjust. There are schools that are mostly run by public funds, where this kind of reasoning might be applicable, and then there are private schools. In most cases though, neither of these two types of schools exclusively use public or private resources. Directly or indirectly, private schools also benefit from public funds or shared resources. Schools might have many reasons to adopt an admission policy, as long as it is just, and in such a system, based upon the merit or the rules, every able student should be qualified and able to compete for admission to the program of his or her choice.

The difficult part is to define what a just admission policy for a school is. After desegregation, admitting black students in colleges was believed to be a just policy. The intended justice of this policy might have benefited many African Americans, but many others, for a different reason, could still not have full or equal access to college or quality education. At elementary and high school levels, the discrepancy gap of monetary resources and the ambient environment became so great, for one reason or another, that the majority of these students remained poorly educated and could not compete in the increasingly competitive college education process. Justice half done, for the affected, culminates in injustice.

Can we pay a woman less than what a man earns for the same job? Discrepancy in salary structure or promotion between men and women is pervasive all across the globe; in some places, it is hidden, and in others, it is the standard practice. Afraid of losing their livelihood, most women can't even start questioning this policy of gross injustice.

Probably, nobody would disagree now that the practice of human slavery over thousands of yesteryears was a grossly unjust and frequently cruel practice. Our dislike and changed attitude toward this practice was probably the direct result of our experience with a better social justice system. The subsequent rewards such a system provided within a society might have led to the effort for its abolishment.

At this time, human slavery, the way it used to be, might still exist in isolation. More widespread is what we may call the modern form of slavery. In the practice of slavery, human beings are exploited, physically and/or emotionally, without appropriate or less-than-appropriate consent and compensation. They are deprived of many basic rights without access to a reasonable system of justice. In extreme cases, they could even become property and a commodity. The effect of these multiple shades of slavery could vary from injustice to cruelty and even beyond. Farm, household, restaurant, and factory work are just a few examples where this kind of practice might be easily found. Sorry to say, it is not limited to just one culture or a few countries. It is much more pervasive.

A father who gets bored and frustrated with the mother of his young child and leaves them alone inflicts injustice on both of them even if he provides some financial support. A mother who indulges in alcohol and/or drugs while ignoring the welfare of her children does the same. An underage or unemployed woman, on a state welfare system, who gets pregnant and bears a child, does not do justice to the people already supporting her. But if that happens and the woman's family or the community ignores providing some reasonable support to the mother and the child, they do the same.

Sometimes, injustice is wrapped in a wreath of apparent generosity. According to a common

Pakistani or Indian tradition, daughters on their wedding day receive a whole series of household items, from twenty-one or any odd number of dresses to expensive electronic appliances, whatever the family can afford at the time of the wedding. It is nothing but an unjust tradition forced upon the bride's family. But what I was alluding to was something different. I am not talking about poor folks who start saving for their daughter's wedding as soon as she is born; I am talking about families with resources in cash, land, businesses, or industrial complexes. Their daughters receive an elaborate dowry at their wedding and continue to receive gifts every time they visit their parents. What they usually don't get is their fair share in the family's estate and resources, contributing to a life of perpetual indignity and injustice for women.

Let's talk about a different topic: fatherless children. A woman, without any relationship with a man, is free to have children, any number of them, by using sperm from a donor, who could remain anonymous in our system. Though it fulfills her desire to have a child, without a father, the child could be at a significant social and legal disadvantage right from the start. It at least doubles the chances that the society or her family might have to bear part of the burden of child care, if something happens to her. Some might say that the same also applies to a man and a woman having a child who might separate and not live together. But the situation is obviously different; in the case of the sperm donor, the father's absence is guaranteed.

Is it unjust if we stop a woman getting pregnant in this manner? If we keep our attention only to that particular woman, it might be. It is after all fair that each woman decides herself about her choice of conceiving a child or not. Could her or any single mother's such action in any way be unjust to her family or the rest of the community? Potentially, it could be. Excluding the fiscal concerns, which are also significantly important in today's living situation, if she has a medical or a psychiatric condition that potentially could also affect her child or if because of such conditions she might not be able to take care of her child, it could be. All such situations might require help from the family or the society at large even if they had no sway on her initial decision. What decision should she or the society make to avoid any injustice to each other? For a number of reasons and people's beliefs, it is difficult to come up with a straight answer to this question. For whose interest should the decision be designed, the child, the mother, or the society? I believe the child is the one without proper representation in this triangle and his or her interests should surpass any others.

If a rare medical condition could be treated by tissue taken from the parents' child and they would like to bear one for that reason, should we encourage or allow this practice? Can a teenager ethically be accepted as a valid blood or organ donor? These and the one above are difficult ethical questions and carry an inherent risk of inflicting injustice on the party not consulted or not able to appropriately consent at the time of such a decision.

Transplanting an organ, like a kidney or cornea, from somebody who has passed away, with the appropriate personal or family consent, is a standard medical practice. In many countries, where laws are less stringent or overlooked, the practice of organ transplantation poses a dilemma. Poor men and women are willing to give away part of their body for money. It does not really matter what amount of money is involved. The fact is they give away part of themselves for cash. What argument can we have against an adult who willingly gives away a pint of blood or one of his kidneys for cash? For the sake of our discussion, when we are concentrating on the concept of justice and injustice, stopping this practice completely might be unjust to the rights of the donor. There are laws, I believe, in most countries where transplant surgery is available to prevent unjust or exploitative practices, but such laws are routinely ignored in many of them. People from more law-abiding or richer areas regularly travel to other less strict or poorer areas to obtain a kidney donation.

An adult willingly donating an organ for the purpose of saving someone else's life does not do any injustice at all, provided the donation does not make the donor sick, disabled, or dependent. Injustice, in this case, is an arrangement between a donor and a recipient, even without any hint of coercion or pressure, agreeing on a material or monetary recompense but without any oversight or rules in place to protect their respective interests. Any such arrangement with the donor without this minimum requirement seems far worse than injustice.

This is not an effort to condone the system of compensation for organ donation. I am trying to explore and understand the complex facets of this practice, which might help us to come up with a just solution both for the donor and the recipient. Incidentally, if we study the present state of organ donation, we might notice that the practice of monetary or material compensation is not universal and is merely a reflection of the general lawlessness and injustice in the affected society.

Another criticism of organ transplantation some people have is an aversion to dismembering or mutilating the human body. Let's look at this issue first in living donors. A kidney removed from my body would only have my genetic identification mark or address. I am really not there. It is not that different from donating a pint of blood, except the kidney does not grow back. What makes a human body sacred is its soul, a concept we are unable to analyze with our scientific means. But maybe we could try to fathom it by just closing our eyes and perceiving our inner self—the self that we cannot see, feel, or touch; the self that would be there even if we lost a limb or two. This entity, the self, does not necessarily need every part of our physical body to survive or thrive; it is just using it as its physical envelope. Once this leaves the body, what remains is only the envelope. Organ donation, if done correctly, does not do any injustice to the soul, the real being.

But this envelope or dwelling for a human soul remains ethically sacred, even long after its use. Its revered status and inviolability is probably coded in our brain. Mutilation of the human body, including self-mutilation, is a universally established aberrant behavior; sometimes, it is due to criminal acts, and in other cases, it is part of psychopathology. Though usually seen and described in individuals, sometimes this behavior may affect or manifest in a group of people. In that case, we might observe some of the most unusually aberrant or bizarre conduct for human beings. People can harm a person or even kill him or her and then may continue to hit or mutilate the dead body. Can people as a group suddenly behave like criminals, or could they develop, what looks like, a psychiatric disorder explaining this type of behavior? Logically speaking, the answer to both questions is affirmative. This type of group behavior, in some situations, might reflect the nature and extent of injustice or cruelty to which they have been exposed. Sustained and widespread injustice in a society may result in a large-scale irrational, brutal, and sometimes even psychotic behavior. It is not uncommon, in some societies, for a group of ordinary-looking people, if they happen to catch a thief or a robber, to manifest this transformative behavior. They may start hitting the suspect, without even asking a question or deliberating, with every other person joining them to the extent that the unfortunate being could very well be critically injured or even killed, unless somebody with a sane mind intervenes. Children raised in this type of environment may never get the chance to hit an adult, like the grownups, but could manifest similar behavior. They could be found hitting or torturing one of their own or an innocent animal—all because of the injustice and cruelty of the system all around them.

What is the real reason that prostitution remains illegal in most areas? Legally speaking, our system does not restrict consenting adults from having sex, even when they are already married. Why then do we frown upon prosti-tution? How does it differ from having an affair with the neighbor's wife or an intern in our office? The social implications of the latter could be even more detrimental. I say we do injustice by punishing a prostitute using the argument of "ethics," while completely ignoring our adult sexual indiscretions with an argument of "freedom."

Prostitution, in fact, is a reflection of the gross injustice of our gender, social, and eco-nomic value system. In most cases, victims are women; many times, they are quite young, often less well educated, and poor. We tend to believe that prosecuting a few women and/or their agents will somehow stop this practice. These actions might only help to diffuse this matter farther into the society. Like poison ivy, it camouflages itself to hide in its surroundings, becoming even more dif-ficult to find and control, but it's right there if you know what you are looking for and where to find it. A better approach might be to address the social and economic issues that bring men and women to this level as well as the reasons for our misguided social behaviors to minimize its demand. Maybe then, we could say that we have tried to reverse this gross injustice.

Do we do injustice to gays and lesbians when we don't legally or morally accept their "marriage"? The discussion here is about marriage and to whom and how one can be declared married. Marriage is an old human institution that allows a man and a woman to be intimate with each other without any social or legal repercussions, live together, have sex, and bear children. The purpose of this institution is to join men and women in couples, establish the foundation of a family, provide a legal framework for the care of the future generation, and decide on matters of inheritance.

Biologically speaking, for a married relationship to start, "she" provides at least an ovary and a uterus, while "he" brings a functional testes and his ability to deliver its contents. Marriage allows these two people to legally and ethically complete the act of bringing a sperm to an egg. A marriage can break apart, and many times it does, if either of these units is found defective.

There are always some exceptions, but they remain exceptions. People may not divorce if one or both partners are unable to conceive or bear a child. A man and a woman might not have any interest in having a child, or they might have some other reasons and motivations for marriage besides sex and children. It is also important to note that legally speaking, in our culture, an unmarried man and woman can live together, have sex, and have children if they want to and do almost everything a married couple would do, except maybe filing a joint tax return.

Gay or lesbian partners don't bring the essentially complementary biological apparatuses to justify a marriage. A couple of ovaries or a set or two of testicles alone do not bear a human life to existence. Their union definitely brings two people together but for a different reward. One can have any appropriate name and classification for this union, but not marriage—at least not the way humans have defined it for centuries. As far as friendships and living partnerships are concerned, there could be multiple reasons and ways people could decide to live together, besides just belonging to the same sex or not even having a defined one. It would be unjust to deprive them of some of the basic rights of friendship and living together just because they are not "married."

Another subject we can analyze to understand the concept of injustice is our interaction and relationship with animals. Animals are an integral part of human development and civilization, both in the field and on the table. As human wit surpassed most of the physical or instinctual advantages animals might carry, our relationship with them has mostly depended upon our needs and circumstances. In modern-day living, machines have taken over the type of workload long performed by animals. To many of us, it might seem unjust or even cruel to think about an animal driving our cart or carriage or animals walking for hours in a circle providing us power to run a machine. Even horseback riding might now be declared questionable if not impractical. Technological development and machines, in fact, have resulted in a remarkably favorable change for the animals in the way we use them or deal with them. On a social level, animals now have "rights," and their maltreatment is scrutinized and sometimes prosecuted. This is a good example of where we have changed our attitudes and policies to minimize injustice and cruelty; we have, in fact, moved in the direction of justice.

In spite of all these changes in our behavior, for practical or volitional reasons, especially in the minds of some of us, we are not doing enough or we continue to be unjust or cruel to animals. We can see that animals are still used in biomedical research. They are still caught, trained, and displayed for our fun and play. Their skin or other body parts are used for clothing or fashion. In some countries, animals, fish, and birds are trapped or hunted, sometimes even at the risk of destroying a whole species. Even the rarest of animals are killed to get the right ingredient for an eccentric remedy or a "gourmet" dish. And finally, to the dismay of some of us, we continue to put animal meat on our dinner table.

Differentiating these behaviors in just and unjust terms sometimes becomes difficult mostly due to the biases we introduce to our analysis.

Anybody could be hostile toward a harmful animal, bird, or even insect, but sometimes there is a widespread systemic dislike and aggressiveness toward animals. One could study this phenomenon comparing the interaction of humans and common birds or animals in different communities. In some places, they could come in close proximity to each other without any sign of fear or anxiety. In others, animals or birds might run or fly away as soon as they smell or catch a glimpse of a human presence. In some other situations, for both humans and animals, proximity to each other is not always beneficial. In fact, sometimes the fear of each other might be the key to maintaining a certain level of separation critical to the existence of a species. In such a case, getting too close or friendly with a particular animal might be detrimental to its or its species' long-term survival and is unjust or even worse.

Unjust acts and policies have larger and longer-lasting effects. An unjust school policy creates imbalanced parallel societies. While one group gets the best possible means of education, the other could be left to a miserable, undignified existence. This is what is happening in a lot of countries around the globe, a significant factor that keeps these countries restive and underdeveloped. To a certain extent, if not of that magnitude, we have the same problem here. We are leaving a whole section of children behind with substandard education. Not unlike any other country in the world, this policy could haunt us in the future; it could create an inharmonious society with a lack of mutual trust and respect. On a more practical level, it could contribute to poverty and a lower standard of living for all of us.

Many talk about democracy and its benefits to a society. In the basic sense, trying to be just for every citizen of a society, democracy guarantees a majority rule while each and every adult individual has an equal say in selecting the leaders and policies. It does not necessarily guarantee a lack of exploitation of minorities, unless the rule of law and a proper code of ethics are followed. There are a number of present-day examples where the so-called democratic societies are responsible for perpetual discrimination against minorities or their rights. Such practices are injustice and cruelty inflicted on a mass scale. Negative effects of these policies reverberate all around the globe, in a way, affecting people living even thousands of miles away.

Understanding the concept of injustice described here is not only important to comprehend the intricacies of our legal system; its expanded approach also helps us in many other areas of our life. A good example is farming. If it is done without any inherent harm to the environment, animals, or the crop itself, the farmer does justice to his job. There is ample evidence to suggest that the so-called "organic" ways of farming produce a better product, if not in excessive quantity. Even a small change in farming practice can significantly alter the product or the surrounding environment. I love peaches, though not the ones in supermarkets that look so big and delicious but taste like sponges. The same can be said about many other fruits and vegetables. A visit to an alternative grocery store might provide a different type of produce, full of aroma and flavor. The differences are many, including genetically

modified seeds, gene or trait selection, fertil-
izers, and chemical insecticides. These factors
can definitely enhance the size and number
of a crop, but at a price, the price of a delicate
balance reached over centuries of farming,
the price of justice to our environment.

Caring for the sick and injured nowadays
is a complicated affair. Gone are the days
when a doctor in the community was all in all,
with an office and a few instruments, providing every type of medical, obstetrical, and
surgical care. Medical care now involves many
more players, including a variety of doctors,
nurses, counselors, hospitals, pharmaceutical
companies, pharmacies, multiple types of
manufacturing businesses, nursing homes,
and the list goes on and on. Besides caring for
the patient, all of these players have their own
distinct interests. In a system like ours, which
runs like a business, growth and monetary
rewards are their usual optimum goals and

the care of patients is only a means to those ends. In spite of some obvious flaws, before we make any significant change in our ways, it might be prudent to study other health-care systems, including their potential expense and pros and cons.

The best part of our health system is that it works well for an individual or a company who can afford to pay a good price. It is not perfect, but it works well. A patient can see any doctor of his or her choice and obtain any indicated medicine or intervention in a timely fashion. This is our way of medicine. We are not trained to wait for a specialist consultation for more than a few days if we have a problem more than a cold or flu. For anything more serious, we expect to be taken care of in a day or two or even earlier. We expect medical interventions to improve our quality of life, not just to heal our sickness or injuries. As the money, most of the time, does not directly come from our pockets, we expect our doctors to look for each and every possible cause and treatment. The whole medical system is geared to cater to these needs.

The worst part of our health system is that it does not work well for the society as a whole. It carries tremendous limitations for those who cannot afford it. This system is designed to take good care of individual patients, not the whole society. It is quite expensive and frequently wasteful. Extending the present individual benefits to all people, including those who cannot pay a fair premium, could be a just cause provided we find a reasonably just way to pay for it.

Health care is a good example to study for our present discussion. The discrepancy in health-care delivery is injustice on a large scale. Its effect is negative both on individuals without coverage and the society in general. To mitigate this problem and to bring it to a just

level, we have to find ways to provide a prede-
termined minimum level of care to everyone.
Subsidizing this coverage for those unable to
afford it is ihsaan, a concept discussed in the
next chapter.

WHAT IS IHSAAN?

*A*s I stated in the introduction, conceptually speaking, there is something that we might consider as better or beyond what we call justice for a particular situation or scenario. In an ideological sense, the position where the expanse of justice ends brings us to the place of ihsaan. It implies an act, policy, philosophy, or ideology that may be considered better than justice. In the context of humanity, it is what elevates one human being above others. Neither mandatory nor obligatory, it is an act better and beyond the realm of justice. To its benefactor, it does not provide mere comfort; it provides an internal peace.

As I try to explain this concept with some commonplace examples, you might agree that with a solid foundation of justice in place, an element of ihsaan may be the basis of a progressive, compassionate, and benevolent person, family, or society. Here, I hope you avoid the usual political connotations of these words. Ihsaan may strengthen our social bonds and, in an emotional and spiritual sense, bring us closer to each other. It may provide the basis to heal and manage some of the most difficult afflictions affecting human beings and the environment.

Unjust and cruel actions, on the other hand, have long-lasting and sometimes permanent negative repercussions. In physical terms, the damage may be obvious or imperceptible. In either case, it could have a detrimental effect on the situation, the subject, the subject's psyche, or the future. Justice may mitigate these negative effects but not undo them. Ihsaan, on the other hand, has the potential to go beyond that level. In a biological sense, there is the possibility that it may trigger certain genes in our brain or turn off some others that could potentially undo the damage inflicted by injustice or cruelty. It may very well bring the brain to a level where it could again be inquisitive, constructive, and productive.

Understanding the concept of ihsaan is somewhat difficult, as, according to my research, it is not well studied or documented. Some examples may help us to grasp its basics. A person with limited physical and/or intellectual ability, by birth, disease, or accident, deserves our attention and consideration. It would be just to provide this person with safety, food, shelter, and treatment for any sickness. Providing the same with empathy and compassion is ihsaan.

This is especially true for our elderly. In a just society, the elderly would have a reliable system of care, a safe and comfortable place to reside, a predictable meal plan, and a nurse or a doctor if they need one. Ihsaan is when this same level of care is provided to those without enough means to pay for it.

Shoveling and sanding our driveway, so that a visitor or a mail carrier can safely enter is justice; shoveling the driveway of a sick or elderly neighbor with no desire for any recompense is ihsaan.

Arriving for work on time and not wasting any during the work hours is the employee's justice to his or her employer. Protecting the employer's interest, on top of putting in the time, is ihsaan. Appropriate compensation for every minute of one's employees' work is justice; paying them when they are sick or pregnant and unable to work is ihsaan. Paying an employee only for the services rendered is justice; giving them a bonus for an unexpected profit is ihsaan.

Teachers, after our parents, probably carry the most important influence upon us. Our success and failure may largely depend upon the quality of their work. They do justice to their work if they carry a proper knowledge of their subject matter and the accompanying skills of teaching, use them in an appropriate manner, and take responsibility for their students' learning. If they provide extra help or guidance for a student who is failing or another who might need a higher level of instruction, it is their ihsaan.

Planting a tree and benefiting from its fruit, shade, or beauty is justice; planting a tree for the benefit of others is ihsaan.

Catching a burglar, retrieving the goods, and putting him or her in jail could very well be justice, but exploring the causes of his or her actions and trying to fix them would be ihsaan.

Migration of human beings, at least for some of them, from their native land to any other is probably instinctual and could be facilitated by a number of factors. It provides a system to bring people from different ideologies and ways of living closer to each other. It is also the vehicle to develop fresh ideas and novel solutions. In spite of all the paranoia and second thoughts, the inclusiveness of our society, which provides the basis for legal migration, is an act of ihsaan. It is our major strength, not a liability.

Any discussion about immigration is incomplete unless we discuss the inequalities of the present-day world. Countries and regions drastically differ in wealth and resources. Geopolitical boundaries, many of them artificially created, add to this problem. Political conflicts and restrictions on trade, business, and communication systems marginalize whole countries. Social discrimination based upon religion or ethnic background can deprive people of a fair share in local resources and opportunities.

Violent crimes against minorities are overlooked and underprosecuted. With all these factors and the ease of travel in the present-day world, immigration, for a large section of the world's population, has become their first option instead of a last resort.

As long as vast inequalities of wealth and resources between nations continue, even for things as simple as a piece of bread and clean water, men and women will continue to depart their homeland and traverse other borders. Treating them with respect, instead of erecting barbed wires around the country, is justice; paying attention to their homeland, sincerely and constructively, and helping them improve their quality of life, is ihsaan.

The ecosystem we live in is maintained by a harmonious interaction of the atmosphere and its contents. To a certain extent, it can handle variations in its chemical composition or physical characteristics, such as temperature. There is a growing body of evidence that this system is reaching its limits with the increasing likelihood of a significant environmental change, which might be detrimental to many islands and countries. The evidence also suggests that a large part of this change, the injustice inflicted on the environment, is caused by us, human beings. We might be just to undo some of this by correcting our ways and controlling our actions, but a meaningful change may not take place until the measures we take reach the level of ihsaan.

For example, Berkshire County in Western Massachusetts is a picturesque place. Here, in the middle of the industrial phase of the last century, factories on the riverside used the local water and natural resources and provided employment to thousands of local residents. Not much attention was paid to the drainage or spillage into the river, which later turned out to be a major environmental disaster.

Certain chemicals in the sludge and the factory site were found to be potentially harmful to humans, fish, and other life forms. After long years of deliberations, the business agreed to a solution or a settlement. Theoretically, how do we even figure out a just solution in this kind of case? Could compensating affected people and parties provide enough justice? For some people, it might, but could it undo any of the damage or injustice done to the river and the local environment? How do we compensate the fish? The damage or injustice to the environment could only be mitigated if the offending parties did a lot more than provide compensation. They would have to either remove or practically neutralize the toxic ingredients in the river and the land and bring them back to their natural state. This would be justice.

In spite of many examples like the above and the knowledge and experience we have gained dealing with them, water, land, and environmental damage caused by industrial and farm waste is rampant in many parts of the present-day world. In some countries, the damage is so widespread and severe that it is almost impossible to completely undo it with current resources and technology. The situation is made even worse by the lack of any significant regulations, oversight, or recourse. Business owners, living in isolated mansions, far away from their businesses or factories, are neither directly affected nor bothered by it. Local residents, animals, and vegetation take the brunt of the devastating effects of this type of injustice and cruelty to the environment and the local ecosystem.

Why should we even care about this problem thousands of miles away? The fact of the matter is that any act of injustice or cruelty does not just have local effects. Its detrimental effects permeate much farther. In the present-day interconnected and inter-dependent world, its effects, directly or indirectly, sooner or later, may reach all of us.

In the example of the river in the Berkshire Valley, justice is what our government has been able to obtain from the offending parties, in cash, efforts, and commitments. To reach a level of ihsaan, these parties would have to provide similar efforts or expertise to contaminated places unrelated to their businesses or responsibility, in this country or any other.

Caring for a relative or a neighbor, like we do for ourselves, is a just cause; accomplishing that anonymously is ihsaan.

Raising one's own children—providing the material means, such as food and shelter—is justice; waking up in the middle of sleep and caring for a baby is ihsaan. Justice is to take full responsibility for the upbringing of our own children; accomplishing that for others' children is ihsaan.

Protecting the rights of birds and animals, such as through laws against cruelty, is justice; protecting the habitat for their future generations is ihsaan.

In a present-day government, the formulation of ideas and implementation of policies are almost never based upon a complete consensus. Differences of opinion are ubiquitous, and protests of some form or fashion, in one way or another, are commonplace. To be clear, for the sake of argument, the merit of a policy or the associated protest may itself be debatable. For an observer, either of them could be just or unjust. What could be a just way to protest an unjust policy? How could one protest an unjust ideology or action of an institution or the government? Not with force, at least not by replicating the same unjust actions we are trying to oppose. A protest accomplished in a peaceful manner is a better and more just solution. How should a government react to a protest? At minimum, a just and lawful response is better than any unjust action. For a government, listening to the protestors' point of view with respect and due consideration is justice. Bringing the appropriate policies in place to avert such problems for the future generations is ihsaan.

Are people who are asking to abolish the death penalty in the case of a premeditated murder unjust to the victim or his/her family? Maybe not! Maybe they are asking us to consider a better alternative, an act of ihsaan.

INJUSTICE, JUSTICE, AND IHSAAN–PUTTING IT TOGETHER

P utting a thought process together or in order requires knowledge and understanding. But the concepts of knowledge and understanding, for human beings, are a paradox. A higher level of knowledge leads to a deeper understanding of what is still not known.

Acquiring the knowledge of the working of the ecosystem and the universe to which we belong is an exceedingly slow process. A key element of this understanding is the appreciation of the interdependence of living and nonliving things. At a basic physical or chemical level, there seems to be little difference between the two. In this discussion, I am mostly concerned with the relationship of humans to each other and everything else. As far as we, the human beings, know, in our surroundings, we have the most advanced ability to analyze an action before it takes place and modify it if we want to. We have also acquired knowledge and technology that has the potential to swiftly and markedly affect our surroundings, negatively or positively. This makes it incumbent upon us to pay attention to our thinking process to avoid actions and policies that could be detrimental to us and our surroundings.

As I have tried to explain, the scope of every action and decision we make is broad, providing us many choices. This is a consideration when we deal with ourselves, our family and friends, our countrymen, or people all over the globe. The same is true when we deal with other forms of life and nonliving entities. It is only up to us, each one of us, individually or as a group, to chart our course and influence this system in a particular way. Each of our actions and decisions has consequences: negative or positive, destructive or productive, and insipid or creative.

How do we teach our children to be constructive, inquisitive, and creative? How do we teach them to act in a just manner and strive for ihsaan? How do we instruct them to attempt a higher level of thinking and action, even beyond ihsaan? The best way is through examples, not a lecture. A system or society based upon just principles provides a basis for these ideas and practices to grow. As adults, what we do in our life and how we deal with our parents, our brothers and sisters, our friends and neighbors, our coworkers, people in the grocery store, those we know and those we do not know, our teachers and preachers, the people who work for us and the people for whom we work, those who speak and look like us and those who are different, and many others who complete our life determine what messages we give to our children.

Justice creates freedom, equality, and peace of mind. Like a plant in the garden that grows and flourishes with just the right mix of light, moisture, and temperature, a just society is a developing, advancing, and prospering society. For an individual, it provides full opportunities for development, exploration, and achievement.

Injustice, on the other hand, leads to exactly opposite results. For individuals, at minimum, injustice brings stress and anxiety. Depending upon the situation, it may lead to depression and helplessness, creating dependent personalities. Lack of justice or the practice of injustice induces or worsens such negative tendencies that might otherwise have stayed hidden, unnoticed, or insignificant. On a larger scale, widespread injustice in a society is detrimental to its self-confidence, its ability to create and prosper, and, ultimately, its capacity to lead.

Governance provides a few people power over their fellow citizens. The nature and amount of this power depends upon the type of government. The power of the government is the basis of an organized and lawful society. In spite of its tremendous advantage, unchecked and unaccountable government power is as harmful to the society as no government at all. In a democratic system of government with a strong, just, and balanced constitution, power is shared, accounted for, and allocated to an elected group of people for a certain period of time. For a society in general, this type of governance is more just than many others known to us.

On a more practical level, for a society's development, democracy, in fact, is just a means, not the goal. Without proper ideals, democracy could just be a slogan, in fact, a very successful one, frequently used by the perpetual ruling class. Unless we look beyond vote counting, when addressing the reasons for a society's failure, we could simply draw erroneous perceptions and false conclusions.

Ihsaan leads to peace and fulfillment, opens the door for discovery and invention, and provides for a creative and contented life. It has the potential to dramatically reverse the negative and causative impacts of injustice or even cruelty. Life based upon ihsaan is peaceful, satisfying, and content. A society practicing ihsaan progresses exponentially—physically, intellectually, and spiritually. Ihsaan produces flowers of exceptional color, shape, and fragrance, each in an accurate complementary proportion.

I postulate that, on an individual level, our actions and policies probably set us on a particular course in life, which is facilitated by the activity or inactivity of certain genes in our brain. Just actions and policies might affect one particular set of genes while unjust actions affect a different one. Similarly, cruelty might have a larger or greater negative impact on the offender's brain. The practice of ihsaan, on the other hand, might have the capacity to radically influence or change the negative impact of injustice and cruelty through a similar mechanism. Which brain areas are triggered or inhibited or which genes are turned on or off by such actions would be an interesting research project. This knowledge could be tremendously important not only for a physician treating individual patients with the effects of such policies but also for the policy makers and in fact all of us. It would not only help us not to practice or enforce such negative actions or policies; it could also create avenues to find better treatment for the affected.

The progress of a country or a society depends upon its cumulative or aggregate justice value, which I call its IJI value, the injustice—justice—ihsaan value (see the appendix). It is an estimate of the quality of interaction between different parts of a society—its citizens, animal life forms, vegetation, natural resources, and land. As the society's values, ideologies, and practices become more and more just, and especially if they tilt toward ihsaan, it progresses, physically and intellectually. On the other hand, if it acts in the opposite direction, it starts to fail and falter, it degrades, and it could ultimately disappear, leaving a few ruins and some historical notes and artifacts.

A good practical example to study is how a society deals with women. Besides the differences in appearance, men and women are dissimilar in many other ways, some quite obvious and some imperceptible. This is one of the reasons that, for example, in sports, they compete separately. Are men better than women in cognitive or leadership abilities? There is no solid evidence for that conclusion. Could there be differences in some specific cognitive skills or traits? It is possible, but large-scale studies to explore this question and especially its potential causes are lacking. Given a fair chance, in most if not all fields of work and performance, women can outperform men or could be at par.

Men and women, in fact, are more alike than different, both biologically and intellectually. Biologically speaking, the presence of their respective sexual organs or more specifically certain hormones makes them develop, act, and behave in ways somewhat different from each other. Within a narrow spectrum, each man has a feminine side and every woman has her masculine side. In a just society, the differences between men and women are understood and cherished, without any prejudice or indignation, and are not exploited. As women are at least about half of any population, ignoring their rights and depriving them of their fair share in the society carries tremendous repercussions. From an economic perspective, the inability to utilize the talents and efforts of half of the population is plain irrational and could be one of the largest hindrances to the development and progress of many societies.

Causes of this disparity are many; paranoid religious behavior, a tribal code of ethics and living, a general lack or inadequacy of the education system, and lack or ineffectiveness of the local legal system to protect its citizens' rights are some of them. In a different kind of example, men, in the name of the larger good of the society, have created policies resulting in gross injustice and cruelty inflicted upon women of present and future generations. In the Chinese experiment of a "one-child" policy, without proper nondiscriminatory laws in place or their implementation, many people have opted to abort, in fact kill, their unborn daughters. Both mothers and their daughters bear the brunt of such unjust and cruel policy.

The pornographic industry, which is not very different from prostitution, thrives on female nudity and their sexual, physical, and emotional exploitation. Its existence and practices are to the benefit and pleasure of mostly men. Here, men have successfully exploited the argument of freedom and freedom of expression to satisfy their own desires and needs.

For the economic and social well-being of a society, it makes perfect sense to fulfill women's rights. They should be given equal opportunity to be born, live, receive an education, and work. This can and should be accomplished with the proper understanding and respect of women and men's individual differences. Justice, as we see, in this regard, in many societies, is long overdue.

The principles discussed above are applicable equally to individuals, families, groups, and nations. As long as our actions are just, individually or as a group, we thrive and progress. As soon as the balance is tilted to the other side, we deteriorate, suffer, and regress. Another point to make here is that oftentimes a superficial analysis of the effects of a certain behavior or policy can be misleading. In many situations, positive or negative effects or their repercussions might not be that apparent or could be delayed.

An example is a dictatorial, nonrepresentative form of government. During the larger part of last century, our government, in absolute contrast to what we accept for ourselves, has supported a number of dictators worldwide. In fact, in some cases, it has purposefully derailed a democratic or a more representative government and maneuvered a dictator of its liking into power. This is all done in the name of short-term national interest, while totally disregarding the long-term repercussions to the respective people and to our own nation. The negative effects of these policies, not felt or expected at the time of their inception, will continue to haunt us for a long time coming, besides causing havoc to the individual nations.

Another interesting observation is that the level of justice, injustice, or ihsaan in a family or a society is usually reflected in its people. Even a brief interaction with a group of people could provide a reasonable snapshot. In a just society, it is not only happiness that we see in its people; we see confidence, hope, and contentment. People stay calm and peaceful, without having any reason to doubt each other's intentions. In this state, their autonomic nervous system, the one that controls their emotions, heart rate, and blood pressure, stays calm and controlled. This peace is noticeable in their eyes, facial expressions, and body language. The hallmark of an unjust society, on the other hand, is a lack of trust between people and a constant doubt about their *real* intentions. In such a society, the distrust pours out through people's gestures, language, and actions. Their autonomic nervous system remains in an erratic mode, creating irregularities of sleep, emotions, and bodily functions. This kind of society, a direct result of widespread injustice, is not a healthy society.

What I have tried to do here is provide a framework to analyze a thought or an action. Numerous provided examples can help us to learn this process and hone our skills so that we are able to use them effectively to navigate throughout our life. It is important to remember that things are seldom black and white and there could be multiple levels of a particular negative or positive concept, action, or policy. Every action or policy, on an individual or a group level, has consequences, some mild or short-term and others that are more severe or long-term.

We should do justice dealing with our children, our families, and ourselves. For their long-term sustenance, even animals, trees, and the land they live on require us to deal justly with them. During recent historical times, in terms of the earth and environment, decades of our unjust and cruel policies and their devastating effects can be seen in our cities, forests, and oceans. Reverting to just policies may help to stop these practices, but the recovery will require us to do more than that.

It will require bringing our commitments and actions to the level of ihsaan. We need to push our thinking and policies in the right direction, the direction of ihsaan and maybe even beyond, i.e., love.

BEYOND
INJUSTICE AND
IHSAAN...

*T*he discussion above by no means encompasses every aspect of human life or his understanding of the universe around him. Also, each of the concepts discussed above, if needed, can be extrapolated further. As I stated above, the purpose for this effort is to discuss a basic conceptual framework. The framework discussed so far is as follows:

	CRUELTY	INJUSTICE	JUSTICE	IHSAAN	

Now just for the sake of argument, it would be interesting to fathom concepts beyond the above parameters, especially beyond cruelty and ihsaan. It is also important to keep in mind that each of these concepts has its own breadth and width. Potentially, we could define different levels of cruelty. For example, slapping a child or breaking his limb, as a punishment for whatever reason, might be examples of different levels of cruelty.

A negative or destructive behavior or ideology beyond what we might consider cruelty crosses a conceptual line, the line separating it from insanity, and thus extends the framework further in that direction:

INSANITY	CRUELTY	INJUSTICE	JUSTICE	IHSAAN

The framework could be extended on the other end too, i.e., beyond ihsaan. Knowing what we learned about ihsaan above, it is intriguing to imagine something better than the best form of ihsaan. It seems initially difficult to envision but a glimpse of it is provided. Usually, a mother's relation and behavior to her child is somewhat different from a father's. In general, a father by and large relates to his children in the sphere of justice and ihsaan. A mother usually goes beyond ihsaan, where a father might also venture, and leaps further into the realm of LOVE:

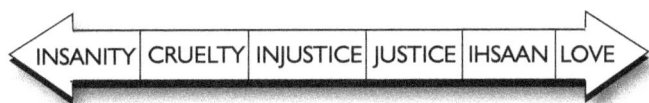

| INSANITY | CRUELTY | INJUSTICE | JUSTICE | IHSAAN | LOVE |

It is enticing to keep on typing and elaborate on cruelty and insanity on one hand and love on the other. The present state of national and international affairs and occurrences makes it especially tempting. But, for now, I have decided to wind up this discussion. I believe a sound understanding of the concepts of justice, injustice and ihsaan is the basis to build up this thinking process further and delve on more complex and difficult to elaborate ones.

APPENDIX

IJI SCORING SYSTEM

*T*his is a proposal to measure a society or a country for its capacity to provide justice to its citizens. The criteria selected is practical but might be, in some aspects, difficult to correctly measure. Each criterion has four scoring points, the higher the better. The best score is 80 and the worst 20.

1. PERSONAL FREEDOM:
CRITICISM OF GOVERNMENT POLICIES

4) No repercussions

3) Covert harassment

2) Overt harassment

1) Jail or punishment

2. RELIGIOUS FREEDOM

4) Complete freedom to practice a reasonable religion

3) Restriction on some reasonable religion(s)

2) General discrimination based upon religion

1) All except one type of religious ideology is suppressed

3. POLITICAL SYSTEM

4) Open democracy

3) Selective democracy

2) Autocratic with elections

1) Autocratic

4. MILITARY

4) Under civilian control with no major involvement in the government

3) Involved somewhat in government affairs but still under civilian control

2) Major involvement in the government with weak civilian control

1) Military dictatorship

5. LANGUAGES

4) All major languages accepted

3) Major language(s) ignored

2) One local language is enforced

1) One foreign language is enforced

6. EDUCATION

4) Free and available to all with equal opportunities

3) Government and private funded with significant difference in quality based upon location or population but available to most

2) Available to less than half of the
population

1) Minimum availability

7. CHILD LABOR

4) None

3) Selective

2) Not frowned upon

1) Essential part of society

8. MINORITY DISCRIMINATION

4) Minimum to none

3) In some areas

2) Subtle and widespread

1) Overt

9. MARRIAGE

4) An individual is free to marry
anybody from the opposite sex

3) Free to marry with family's
permission

2) No marriage outside a particular
sect, tribe, or race

1) No marriage outside family

10. DIVORCE

4) Available with a system in place for
alimony and child care

3) Available with limited system in
place for alimony and child care

2) Generally not available

1) May result in harm to divorcee(s)

11. WOMEN'S RIGHTS

4) Generally, same rights and practices
as for men

3) Allowed to vote, get higher
education or employment, but some
rights are curtailed

2) Allowed to vote but higher education
and employment is restricted

1) Voting is limited or none

12. RAPE

> 4) Fully punished by law
>
> 3) Systematic bias for the victim
>
> 2) Most cases are not punished
>
> 1) Family or system can further harm the victim

13. TREATMENT OF ELDERLY

> 4) Most elderly live in their own homes or with their families with access to health care
>
> 3) Most elderly live in reasonably safe institutions with access to health care
>
> 2) Most lack access to a safe place of residence and/or health care
>
> 1) Minimal system and/or limited traditions for care

14. ANIMAL RIGHTS

> 4) System and traditions exist to prevent animal abuse

3) Animal abuse laws are generally
   ignored
2) No laws for animal abuse prevention
1) Majority of animals are malnourished,
   abused, or dying

15. ENVIRONMENT AND LAND

4) Protected by laws and good practices
3) Limited laws and traditions or their
   implementation
2) Minimum laws and traditions or
   their implementation
1) No laws or traditions for protection

16. CLEAN WATER FOR DRINKING AND HOUSEHOLD USE

4) Available to most of the population
3) Available to the majority of
   the population
2) Selective availability
1) Most places lack this facility

17. PLUMBING

 4) Most places have proper plumbing

 3) Majority have proper plumbing

 2) Selective places have proper plumbing

 1) Most places lack proper plumbing

18. TREATMENT OF PEOPLE WITH NO WELL-DEFINED GENDER

 4) Equal member of society with no discrimination

 3) Selective areas with discrimination and intolerance

 2) Widespread covert discrimination and intolerance

 1) Widespread overt discrimination and intolerance

19. HEALTH SYSTEM

 4) Good quality system easily available to all citizens

3) Wide availability, poor quality

2) Selective availability

1) Minimal availability or very poor quality

20. OUTDOOR SAFETY

4) Generally safe day and night

3) Generally unsafe at night

2) Generally unsafe for children or women alone

1) Generally unsafe

NOTES

NOTES

www.ingramcontent.com/pod-product-compliance
Lightning Source LLC
Chambersburg PA
CBHW031322040426
42443CB00005B/184